Lawler Education → *Adult Skills*

MORE SKILLS FOR LIFE

Judith Parfitt B.Ed., Cert. Ed.,
Adv. Dip. Educ

MORE SKILLS FOR LIFE

Judith Parfitt

The author's rights have been asserted.

978-1-84285-419-8

Reprinted 2017

Produced and Published by
Lawler Education
Lamorna House
Abergele
LL22 8DD
www.graham-lawler.com
Lawler Education is a division of GLMP Ltd

© 2016 Lawler Education ... ay copy these pages for use in their own school.

MORE SKILLS FOR LIFE

Number/General Thinking Series
Introducing Algebra 1: Number Patterns and Sequences
Introducing Algebra 2: Specialising and Generalising
Introducing Algebra 3: Introducing Equations
Introducing Algebra 4: Equations and Graphs
Number Machines
Writing and Forming Numbers

Aussie Tales: Developing Morals and Values in KS2 and KS3/P1–6/S1–3
Teaching Guide
Blubber and Floss
Jimmy and the Blue Bottles
Macca Dacca
Magpie Madness
No Presents for Christmas
Ratbags
Shape Shifters
The Copperhead
The Crossover
The Football

Aber Education Teacher Books
Family Relationships
Bullying and Conflict
Hey Thompson
Self-esteem and Values
Self-esteem: a manual for mentors
Enhancing Self-esteem in the adolescent
Grief, illness and other issues
Survival Teen Island: The Ultimate survival Guide for teenagers

Self-Help
Choose Happiness
The Eat well stay slim budget cookbook
Write yourself Well

English
Creativity through Language 1: How to Teach Fictional Writing
Creativity through Language 2: How to Teach Informative/Non-Fictional writing
Reading for Comprehension 1

5006295

Cross Curricular
Titanic: The Story of a Tragedy

Financial Literacy/Capability
Back to the Black for Primary Schools

Adult Skills/ Skills for Life
Spelling
Cloze
Cloze: Cars and Transport
Reading Comprehension
Guided Reading and Writing
Punctuation
More Punctuation
Family Life
Life Skills
More Life Skills
Applications and Forms

www.graham-lawler.com

Many more titles in development

The worksheets for the students and the other activities are on the disc.

£20 Lawler Education Voucher for detailed and complete reviews.
The purpose of this form is to give you, the teacher, an opportunity
for improvement/positive feedback.

Resource Name_____ Resource ISBN_____

Your Name_____ Your Position _____

School Name_____

Address _____

_____

Overall, what do you think about this resource ? _____

_____

_____

How does it help your students ?_____

_____

_____

What could you say to a colleague in a neighbouring school to persuade them to use this resource ?

_____

_____

How well does it match the specification and which specification is it ? _____

_____

Other Comments, suggestions for improvement, errors, please give the page number

_____

Resources I would like published

Resources I might like to write, or have written, for consideration for publishing.

Fax: 01745 826606   email: info@graham-lawler.com
post: Lawler Education, Lamorna House, Abergele LL22 8DD

Tutor Notes
The purpose of the learning activities in this book is to help students to identify and spell and use the names of things in the environment around the home.

Session One

Aim
To develop language based around the home.

Learning Outcomes
At the end of this session the student should be able to:
- use the language of the home in context,
- spell those words correctly.

Introductory Activity
A good starting point is to hand out pictures from magazines showing outdoor life at home. Ask the students to talk about the pictures and use it as a formative assessment opportunity.

Main Activity
Use pp 1 powerpoint/open office slide show. This is an opportunity to engage students in using language.

Now would be a good time to use the smartboard anagram games. These should also work on non-Smartboard boards. There are three versions of the same activity, namely fast, medium and slow and there are three versions without images.

Plenary
Ask the students to complete *This Old House* and *Parts of a House* worksheets. You may wish to use

On the Radio as an assessment vehicle.

Name_____

1. One of these houses is made of wood, the other of brick.

| This house is made of _____ | This house is made of _____ |

2. My house/flat is made of _____

3. Where is the roof on this house?

Draw an arrow to show where the roof is, on this house.

4. A roof can be covered in different materials. Usually they are covered in tiles but sometimes in thatch, which is straw or reeds.

This roof is covered with

This roof is covered with

_____

_____

Name_____

1. It is the place where people enter the house. In Britain it usually opens inwards but in other European countries it usually opens outwards. It is called the _____

2. It is on the roof, it allows smoke from the fire to escape and keeps the room smoke free.
It is called the _____

3. It is built into the walls and allows light into the room. It can also usually be opened to allow fresh air into the room.
It is called the _____

4. Around a home you will see the roof over-hangs the walls. This area is called the eaves. Houses have eaves because _____

Imagine you are a radio presenter interviewing a guest.

Chat with another person, and describe where you live. Try and use the words we have discussed in this session.

Record your conversation on a phone or other recording device. You may be asked to download the conversation for your tutor to assess your progress.

When you are having your chat try and use open questions rather than closed questions. Closed questions are questions that can be answered with a 'yes' or 'no'.

' Are you happy?' is a closed question because we can answer 'yes' or 'no'.

Open questions are questions that start with what, where, why, when and how. These are often called 'WH' questions even though 'How' does not start with a WH.

Try asking ' WH' questions since they cannot be answered as 'yes' or 'no'.

' Where do you live?' means you are asking a question that needs more than a yes or no answer.

Don't forget to record your chat.

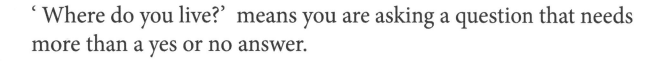

The World at One is a BBC news programme every weekday lunchtime.
Go to the BBC Iplayer and go to the on demand section, here you can hear real radio interviews.

The woman in the photo above is Martha Kearney a highly rated journalist. She is not the only presenter on WATO (World at One).

Look for WATO on Twitter and other social media.

Are the interviews straightforward and easy to understand ?

What kind of questions does the presenter ask ?

Write or record a report on what you have heard.
Say how they asked the questions, what words did they use to start the questions?

Could you be a radio interviewer ?

If yes say why you would be good, if no, say why not.

Aim
To develop language based around the home.

Learning Outcomes
At the end of this session the student should be able to:
- use the language describing the outside of the home in context,
- spell those words correctly.

Introductory Activity
Ask students how many have a garden. If they do have a garden ask them to describe it. If they do not, e.g. flat dwellers, ask them to describe a public garden.

Ask students to discuss these questions in pairs and write down their answers:
- What type of gardening do you like?
- How much time do you spend in the garden?
- What are the names of some famous U.K. gardens? e.g. RHS Wisley, t.v. presenter Monty Don's *Long Meadow*
- Which vegetables do you grow in your garden?
- What are the names of common U.K. flowers?
- What do you need to do in the garden in Spring?
- Would you prefer a flower garden or kitchen garden and why?
- What do you think about organic gardening?

Main Activity
Ask students to complete *In the Garden* and *Outside My Home*

Plenary
Ask the students to complete the gardening crossword. Ensure they are aware that some clues are two word answers and will have a space between the words.

Name_____

Look at these things found outside the house.
Underneath each picture is its name.

lawn   gate   patio

clothes dryer   garden   garage

Write a sentence about each area shown.

_____

_____

_____

_____

_____

Name_____

People like to put things outside their house that makes the space personal.   Write a sentence about each of these things.

BBQ   Outside table   patio chair

kitchen garden   garden pond   water hose

_____

_____

_____

_____

_____

_____

Across

3. area of grass in the garden
6. an outside chair for sitting in the garden
8. can be shortened to BBQ
9. place which contains water in the garden
10. place in the garden to grow vegetables
11. used for eating off when we have a summer meal in the garden

Down

1. used to hang out washing for it to dry
2. hard standing area usually on paving stones
4. Outside building to keep the car in
5. marks the entrance into and out of the garden and can be open or closed
7. long tube to carry water from the tap to where it is needed

Session Three

Aim
To develop language based on jobs around the home.

Learning Outcomes
At the end of this session the student should be able to:
- use the language describing the outside of the home in context,
- spell those words correctly.

Introductory Activity

Ask the students to name their favourite and least favourite task around the home.

Main Activity
Ask students to form and offer sentences using these phrases. Record their offerings either in writing or in audio.

mowing the lawn	hanging out the washing	washing the car
painting the house	weeding the garden	cooking a BBQ
picking flowers	having a swim	planting vegetable seedlings

Plenary
Ask the students to work through *Asking Questions, Say what you see* and *Inside the home.*

Name_____

1. People like to do all sorts of work around their house. What are these people doing? *Choose an answer from below and write your answer underneath each picture.*

mowing the lawn   hanging out the washing washing the car
painting the house   weeding the garden   cooking a BBQ
picking flowers   having a swim   planting vegetable seedlings

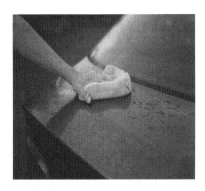

Name_____

1. This house is made out of

_____.

2. This house has a _____roof.

3. This house doesn't have a _____.

4. The _____is made from glass.

5. There _____eaves on this house.

6. There are _____to the door.

7. There is a _____ up to the house.

8. This house has flowers in the

_____.

9. This house has some green

_____ by the front door.

10. There is a _____ to the right
of the house.

1. This house has a _____roof.

2. This house has a _____ under
the front window.

3. This house has a wooden front ____.

4. The house has ____ windows in the
front.

5. This house has a_____
next to the front door.

6. This house has a green _____ on both
sides of the path.

7. This house has not got a _____
for a car.

8. There is a _____ going
to the front of the house.

9. I like this house/ do not like this
house because _____

_____

10. This house is made of _____

Name_____

Look at the pictures below, write down what the people are doing.

_____

_____

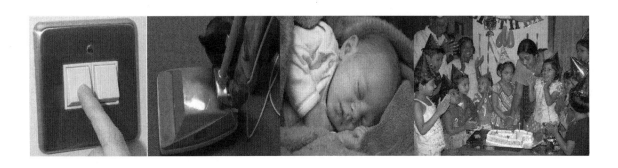

_____

_____

_____

_____

_____

Aim
To develop language based on the home.

Learning Outcomes
At the end of this session the student should be able to:
- use the language describing the outside of the home in context,
- spell those words correctly.

Introductory Activity
Discuss the layout of homes with students.

Main Activity
Ask the students to complete *The Lounge*, *The Bathroom* and *More on the Bathroom* worksheets.

Plenary
Ask the students to write down the labels and next to the name to define them.

Name_____

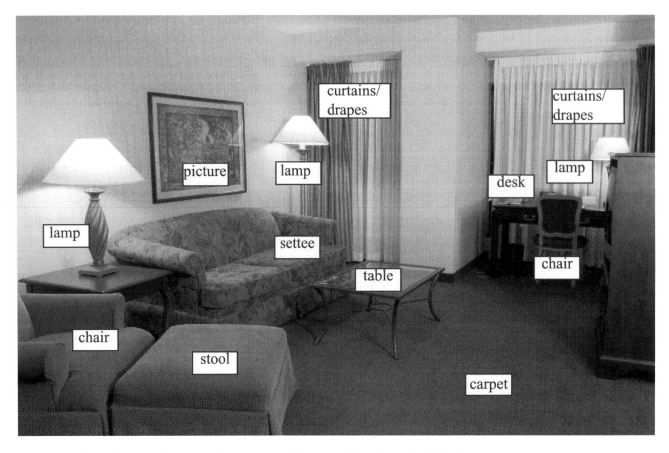

Have a look at this hotel room. The items in the room have been labelled.

Each of these sentences has a word missing. Take a word from the photograph to complete the sentence.

I. The image on the wall is called a _____.

2. The chair that can seat two people is called a _____.

3. Drapes are another word for _____, they hang and cover the windows for privacy.

4. There is a small _____ to put coffee cups on.

5. Sometimes business people stay in this hotel room so there is a _____ for them to work on.

6. To the left of the picture on the table there is a _____.

7. Covering the floor there is a nice _____.

8. Next to the chair on the left, there is a _____ on which you can rest your feet.

Name_____

This is part of a luxury bathroom.

1.   The _____ is the place to get a fast all over wash.

2.   It takes longer but a leisurely soak in the _____ is great.

3.   The _____ and walls are tiled and look great.

4.   On the left hand side you can the _____.

5.   In the picture you cannot see the _____ and that is something every bathroom should have, for personal comfort.

Name_____

1. *Match the object with why you use it.*

a) bath mat   so I can see my face when I'm washing it, or shaving.

b) shampoo   so I won't get smelly under my arms.

c) mirror   so I can wash my face.

d) towel   so I can get all the knots out of my hair.

e) deodorant   so I don't slip over when I get out of the bath or shower.

f) razor   so I can clean my teeth.

g) flannel   so I can dry my body after a bath or shower.

h) toothpaste   so I can dry my hands after I've washed them.

i) comb   so I can clean my hair.

j) hand towel   so I can shave my face, legs or armpits.

2. Below is a list of things we do in the bathroom.

Write a sentence, or sentences, about each one, showing what you need, and how you do it.

a) washing your hair	
b) taking a shower	
c) cleaning your teeth	
d) cleaning your teeth	
e) shaving	
f) having a bath	
g) washing your hands	
h) hanging up towels	
i) moisturising	
j) having a bubble bath	

3. Explain why light switches in the bathroom are on a pull-chord.

_____

_____

_____

Aim
To develop language based outside the home.

Learning Outcomes
At the end of this session the student should be able to:
- use the language describing the outside of the home in context,
- spell those words correctly.

Introductory Activity
Talk through the role of food preparation in the kitchen, stressing the need for hygiene.

Main Activity
Ask students to complete *The kitchen*, *Inside the kitchen* and *The food Cupboard* worksheets.

Plenary
Ask the students to complete *The Cooker* OR *The Pantry* in pairs.

Name_____

Each part of the house has a different function.
Here we are looking at the kitchen.

1.   The kitchen is used to prepare _____ for meals.

2.   The _____ is used to heat food very quickly.

3.   The _____ above the oven is to extract cooking smells.

4.   The place where we wash dirty dishes is called the _____.

5.   The _____ on the wall is used for storage.

6.   On the work surface next to the microwave there is a _____, it is used to prepare
        vegetables.

7.   Next to the sink you can see a _____, it is used to boil water for tea.

8.   The _____ is used for cooking roast meat dishes like roast lamb and curry dishes

Name_____

1. Here is a fridge-freezer. *Finish these sentences:*

a) I use the freezer to _____ .

I keep these things in the freezer:

_____ _____

b) I use the fridge to

_____

I keep these things in the fridge:

_____ _____

Did you notice the eyes on the food, this stops people raiding the fridge to 'snack'.

Name_____

Most kitchens have at least one food cupboard.

1. What can you see on the second shelf on the left with organic in the name?

_____

2. What are the small bottles on the stand on the left of the lower shelf?

_____

3. Name one thing you can find in your kitchen cupboard.

_____

Name_____

oven grill   elements
controls   stove door
grill door

1. Label each part of the cooker

2

i) I use the _____ to cook my vegetables.

ii) I sit pies on the _____ in the oven.

iii) I use the _____ for baking and roasting.

iv) I need a _____so I know how hot to cook food.

v) I need a _____so I can bake a cake.

vi) I have _____which I put pots on to cook our vegetables.

vii) I use the _____ so I can make the pots boil or simmer.

3. What do these words mean?

Write down a definition for each one.

baking _____

roasting _____

boil _____

simmer _____

    27

Name_____

In a house there are several places to store food. One place is a cupboard or pantry. Other food items need to be kept chilled or frozen. They are put in a fridge and a freezer or a fridge-freezer.

1. What is a pantry? You can put lots of _____ items into this big cupboard.

2. What do you think are in the bottles on the floor of the pantry?

_____

_____

3. On the top shelf there is a cylinder shaped object. This is a metal cylinder with an electrical wire to plug into the mains. Inside the cylinder is a ceramic cooking pot. It is called a slow cooker. What do you think a slow cooker is used for?

_____

_____

4. On the third shelf down from the top, there are some spray containers. What could these be?

_____

_____

_____

5. What brand of spray cleaner do you use?

_____

_____

_____

Aim

To develop language based in the kitchen.

Learning Outcomes

At the end of this session the student should be able to:

- use the language describing the outside of the home in context,
- spell those words correctly.

Introductory Activity

Ask the students to name as many different items from the kitchen as they can.

Main Activity

Ask them to complete the worksheets.

Plenary

Ask the students to complete *The kitchen* crossword. (This is a separate file on the disc). Make sure students are aware that some answers will need a vacant space since they are 2 words eg cheese grater.

Name_____

The photograph shows some kitchen utensils.

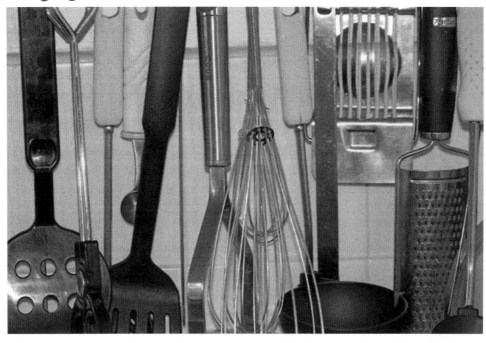

1. Draw lines from these labels to the items in the photograph.

| Cheese Grater | Whisk | Serving Spoon | Egg Slicer |

2.

Why are some cooking utensils like this one, made from wood?

_____

_____

_____

_____

_____

Name_____

Complete the paragraph by filling in the gaps.

When I get up in the morning I like a glass of fresh _____ bought directly from our local farm shop. Later in the morning I like a cup of _____. People are amazed that although I drink milk, I like coffee without _____. I do like a small amount of sugar in my coffee so I

need a _____ from the cutlery drawer.

For lunch I have a veggie _____. This is a healthy alternative to eating meat.

Then in the evening I cook a meal for myself which is usually a veggie_____ or a fish meal.

Insert these words in the right place.

coffee, milk, spoon, meal, burger

Name_____

1. In list A are some things you would find in the kitchen. List B tells how they are used.
Match them up.

A	B
a) tap	I cut up my food with these and to put food in my mouth.
b) fridge	This stops water running down the sink.
c) pantry	This keeps food cool and fresh.
d) cutlery	I can use it to bake potatoes.
e) sink	I use it to put food on when I'm ready to eat.
f) freezer	It gives me hot or cold water.
g) plug	I fill this up with water to do the dishes.
h) oven	I use it to keep tins and bottles of food in.
i) crockery	I use this to keep food frozen.

2. *Look at the list below. Write beside each one where you would put it in the kitchen.*

a) dog food _____

b) frozen meat_____

c) eggs _____

d) baked beans _____

e) pasta _____

f) knives _____

g) milk _____

h) spoons _____

3. Sarah is doing the dishes. *Read through the sentences below. What will she do first? Put a number beside each sentence to show when she would do it. The first one has been done.*

☐ She puts dish washing detergent in the hot water and puts the rack out on the kitchen top.

☐ She uses a tea towel to dry all the clean dishes.

☐ She wipes down the surfaces and puts the rack away.

☐ She washes all the dirty dishes.

☐ She puts all the dry dishes away in cupboards and drawers.
Match the name of each item to its picture.

fridge-freezer

corkscrew

whisk

Aim

To develop language based outside the home.

Learning Outcomes

At the end of this session the student should be able to:

- use the language describing the outside of the home in context,
- spell those words correctly.

Introductory Activity

We suggest you approach this topic with caution. Some students are from very conservative backgrounds and the implication of intimate relationships may be embarrassing.

As an introduction we suggest that you consider *The Teenage Bedroom* as a safe topic.

Main Activity

Read through *Bedroom Vocabulary* and *More in the Bedroom* with the students and ask them to complete the worksheets.

Plenary

Try some of the online word games with the students.

Name_____

My mum said I can plan to decorate my room. So where do I start, I need paint but first I will need to work out the area of the walls.

I.   Explain how to work out the area of the walls of a bedroom.

_____

2.   Name three things that a teenage girl will need to store in her bedroom.

a _____

b _____

c _____

3.   If a litre of paint covers 10 m², how much paint is needed to paint a room with 25 m² of wall space.

_____

Name_____

My daughter's bedroom has been decorated.

1   Her wardrobes are used to hang _____.

2   Her underclothes are kept in _____.

3   She has a _____ on the left where she can do her school homework.

4   Her drawer units are on _____ to help her move them around the room.

Use these words to fill in the gaps:

drawers   casters   desk   clothes.

Name_____

I. The bedroom is where you sleep. Match up the objects in the bedroom with their names.

bed	bedside table	alarm clock	bed clothes
lamp	pillows	photos	carpet
windows	bathroom	electric plug socket	plant

2.

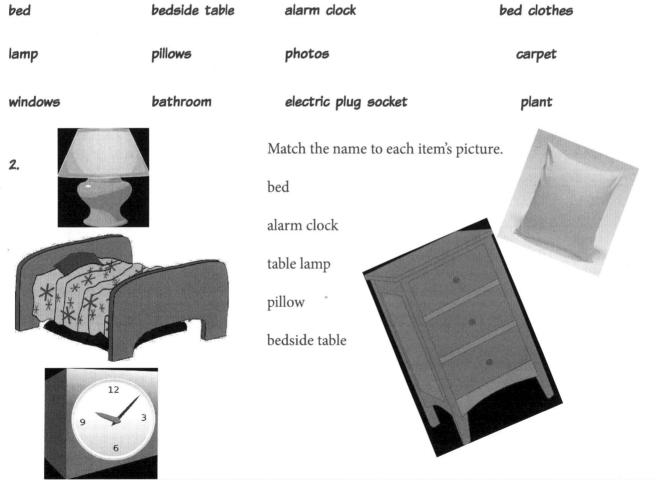

Match the name to each item's picture.

bed

alarm clock

table lamp

pillow

bedside table

Name_____

Look at the picture

a) Put a tick on everything you have in your bedroom. Write sentences for 6 of them.

b) Name everything you can in the picture.

_____

_____

_____

_____

_____

_____

_____

These sites had wordgames that were suitable for students on the day we visited. We strongly advise that you check these sites BEFORE using them in the classroom as the nature of the material may have changed. You also need to play the game and ensure it is British English.

Funbrain: Word Games Online for Kids, Teachers & Parents
http://www.funbrain.com/words.html

Free word games at The Problem Site
http://www.theproblemsite.com/word-games

Vocabulary: This site is stuffed full of games
http://www.vocabulary.co.il/

Sight Words (for 3 to 7 year olds, may be suitable for entry level students)
http://www.education.com/games/reading/sight-words/

also
Sight Words
http://www.primarygames.com/langarts/sightwords/

also
Fun Learning Games
http://www.thekidzpage.com/learninggames/online-word-games/

Reading Games
http://www.primarygames.com/reading.php

Interactive English Games
http://www.funenglishgames.com/games.html

Word Games
http://www.wordgames.com/
Does 'what it says on the tin'.

Aim
To develop more language based on the home.

Learning Outcomes
At the end of this session the student should be able to:
- use the language describing the home in context,
- spell those words correctly,

Introductory Activity
Ask students to consider the uses of rooms in homes. Some rooms are, as we shall see, used as work spaces.

Main Activity
Discuss the dining room and the lounge with students and ask them to complete the respective worksheets.

Plenary
Ask the students to read through working from home and write the letter of application.

Name_____

salad bowl

salad tongues

tumblers

plates

cutlery

chairs

jug

I. This is the dining room where we eat meals.

Draw arrows from the list on the right to name the items on the table,

2. Answer these questions.

a) Do you know how to set a table? _____

b) Is your dining room in the same room as the lounge and/or kitchen? _____

c) What does your dining table get used for, besides meals? _____

_____

d) What other rooms do you eat meals in? Which meal do you eat in which room? _____

_____

e) Have you been out to dinner at a friend's house? Which room did you eat in?

Name_____

seat　　　　coffee table　　　　mirror　　　　settee　　　carpet
window　　　picture cushion　　wooden floor　　light　　　　　waste bin

1. This is the lounge where we relax in the evening. Draw arrows from the list above to where the items are in the photograph.

2. What things do you have in your lounge or sitting room that are missing here ?

_____

3. What activities do you do to relax in the evening ? _____

4. Do you drink coffee in your lounge ? _____

5. What type of music do you find relaxing ? _____

Name_____

Office chair   carpet   desk   computer-keyboard

computer-monitor   notice board   CPU (Computer box)

Lots of people now work from home. Draw arrows from the list to the items in the room.

Answer these questions.

1.   Do you have an office or study at home, to work in or study in? _____

2.   What type of computer do you use? _____

3.   Who do you host your email account with, e.g. Talk-talk, Virgin etc.

        _____

Name _____

Customer Service Representative Bristol

Your role will be 100% phone based and we'll need you to take inbound sales calls from potential new customers, calls from customers who already have a policy...

Applications Solution Architect (Solution Architect) Reading

Microsoft has a flexible working culture and on an average week your time could be split between the office, customer locations and working from home....

Software Specialists – Part Time positions

a Software company - London £30,932 - £44,954 a year

We would also welcome applications from individuals from a non-development bacground, for example IT support....

These are three real jobs that were advertised on the day we looked, online.

Go online: look for home based jobs in your geographical area.

Make a list of the jobs you think that:

a   you could be successful,

b   you think you would enjoy.

Name_____

Aber Antiques are looking for a shop assistant for their antiques shop in Aberford. Knowledge of antiques is not important but a pleasant manner and good relations with customers are vital. Applications in writing only please to Mr A. N. Teak via email to anteak@aberantiques.co.uk

Write a letter of application for this job. Say why you would like the job and explain what you could bring to the job.

This old House p 6

1	wood brick	2	student's own answer (soc)
3	on the top of the house	4	tiles thatch

Parts of a House

1   front door   2   chimney   3   window
4   keeps rain away from walls.

Asking Questions

planting seeds   painting   weeding garden
BBQ   mowing lawn   having a swim
washing car   picking flowers   hanging washing

Say What You See

1. This house is made out of **WOOD**.

2. This house has a **TILED** roof.

3. This house doesn't have a **CHIMNEY**.

4. The **DOOR** is made from glass.

5. There **ARE** eaves on this house.

6. There are **STEPS** to the door.

7. There is a **PATH** up to the house.

8. This house has flowers in the **GARDEN**.

9. This house has some green **SHRUBS** by the front door.

10. There is a **TREE** to the right of the house.

1. This house has a **SLATE** roof.

2. This house has a **SEAT** under the front window.

3. This house has a wooden front **DOOR**.

4. The house has **SIX** windows in the front.

5. This house has a **TREE** next to the front door.

6. This house has a green **LAWN** on both sides of the path.

7. This house has not got a **SPACE** for a car.

8. There is a **PATH** going to the front of the house.

9. I like this house/ do not like this house because **STUDENTS ANSWER**

10. This house is made of **BRICK**.

Inside the home

painting,   cleaning,   washing, switching on plug, vacuuming, sleeping, praying.

The Lounge

1 picture 2 settee 3 curtains   4 table   5 desk 6 lamp 7 carpet 8 stool

The Bathroom

1. Shower   2 bath   3 floor   4 basin   5 toilet

1. *Match the object with why you use it.*

a) bath mat	so I don't slip over when I get out of the bath or shower.
b) shampoo	so I can clean my hair.
c) mirror	so I can see my face when I am washing it or shaving it
d) towel	so I can dry my body after a bath or shower.
e) deodorant	so I won't get smelly under my arms.
f) razor	so I can shave my face, legs or armpits.
g) flannel	so I can wash my face.
h) toothpaste	so I can clean my teeth.
i) comb	so I can get all the knots out of my hair.
j) hand towel	so I can dry my hands after I've washed them.

The Kitchen p22

1.   The kitchen is used to prepare **FOOD** for meals.

2.   The **MICROWAVE** is used to heat food very quickly.

3.   The **COOKER HOOD** above the oven is to extract cooking smells.

4.   The place where we wash dirty dishes is called the **SINK**.

5.   The **CUPBOARD** on the wall is used for storage.

6.   On the work surface next to the microwave there is a **CUTTING BOARD**, it is used to prepare vegetables.

7.   Next to the sink you can see a **KETTLE**, it is used to boil water for tea.

8.   The **OVEN** is used for cooking roast meat dishes like roast lamb and curry dishes

Inside the Kitchen p23

1a) freeze foods, then student's examples   b) keep food fresh   student's examples

The Food Cupboard

1 organic corn starch   2 condiments   3 student's own choice

The Cooker p25

The Cooker cont'd p25

i) elements   ii) shelf   iii) oven   iv) recipe   v) cake tin   vi) stove top vii) controls

baking = to harden by heat in an oven or fire
roasting = to cook by exposure to oven fire/heat
boil = where a liquid is heated to extreme temperature to cook a food
simmer= to cause to boil gently
 definitions courtesy of Collins Shorter English Dictionary

The Pantry
1 grocery 2 beer 3 to cook food slowly and in doing, enhance the taste 4 cleaning products

Kitchen Utensils

2 Some utensils are made of wood because wood is a poor conductor of heat.

Cloze p29

When I get up in the morning I like a glass of fresh **MILK** bought directly from our local farm shop. Later in the morning I like a cup of **COFFEE**. People are amazed that although I drink milk, I like coffee without **MILK**. I do like a small amount of sugar in my coffee so I need a **SPOON** from the cutlery drawer.
For lunch I have a veggie **BURGER**. This is a healthy alternative to eating meat.
Then in the evening I cook a meal for myself which is usually a veggie **MEAL** or a fish meal.

Kitchen Match Up

A	B
a) tap	It gives me hot or cold water.
b) fridge	This keeps food cool and fresh.
c) pantry	I use it to keep tins and bottles of food in.
d) cutlery	I cut up my food with these and to put food in my mouth.
e) sink	I fill this up with water to do the dishes.
f) freezer	I use this to keep food frozen.
g) plug	This stops water running down the sink.
h) oven	I can use it to bake potatoes.
i) crockery	I use it to put food on when I'm ready to eat.

2. Look at the list below. Write beside each one where you would put it in the kitchen.

a) dog food **PANTRY/CUPBOARD** **b)** frozen meat **FREEZER** **c)** eggs **FRIDGE**

d) baked beans **PANTRY/CUPBOARD** **e)** pasta **PANTRY/CUPBOARD**

3. Sarah is doing the dishes. *Read through the sentences below. What will she do first? Put a number beside each sentence to show when she would do it. The first one has been done.*

1 She puts dish washing detergent in the hot water and puts the rack out on the kitchen top.

3 She uses a tea towel to dry all the clean dishes.

5 She wipes down the surfaces and puts the rack away.

2 She washes all the dirty dishes.

4 She puts all the dry dishes away in cupboards and drawers.

Planning to Decorate

1   Walls are rectangles so it is length x height   3 2.5 tins

A Teenager's Room

1 clothes   **2** drawers   **3** desk   **4** casters

The Dining Room p38, the salad tongues are located on the top of the bowl of salad.

Gardening Crossword p 12

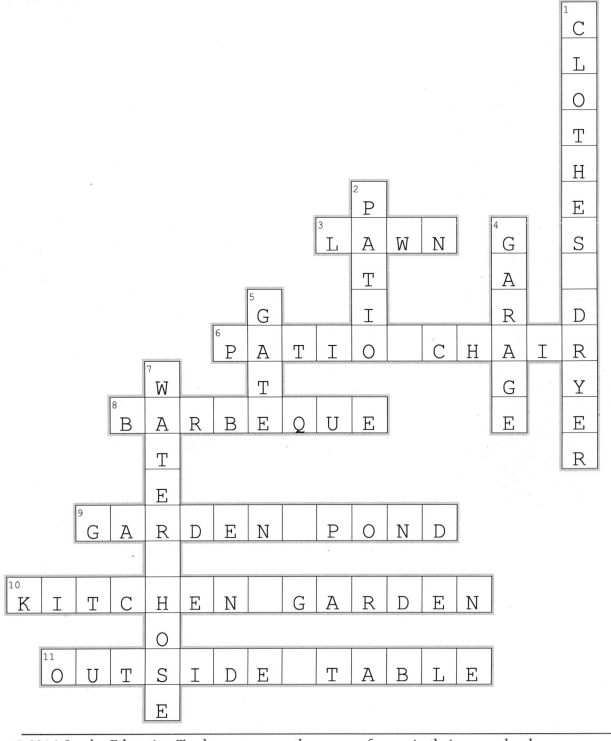